Dear Laverne,

Lean not on your own understanding, but in all your ways acknowledge Him and He will direct your path.   Prov 3-4+5

Love You,

L

www.Thirtydayswithjesus.com

P0/5

30 Days with Jesus
A Prophetic Word from Our Lord and Savior

Evangelist Bernadette Schmitt

authorHOUSE

AuthorHouse™
1663 Liberty Drive, Suite 200
Bloomington, IN 47403
www.authorhouse.com
Phone: 1-800-839-8640

© 2009 Evangelist Bernadette Schmitt. All rights reserved.

No part of this book may be reproduced, stored in a retrieval system, or transmitted by any means without the written permission of the author.

First published by AuthorHouse 4/7/2009

ISBN: 978-1-4389-4339-8 (sc)

Printed in the United States of America
Bloomington, Indiana

This book is printed on acid-free paper.

Introduction

Beloved Reader,

You are about to read a most unusual book. The Lord, Jesus, came to wake me up in the early morning hours to speak about things that have already happened, things that are yet to come, things of heaven and of hell. This began in 2007.

I urge you, if you have not already done so, to pray the prayer you will find at the beginning of this book, to receive the Lord Jesus into your heart.

You will receive and understand so much more from what the Lord desires to show you from this wonderful work He has done when your Spirit Man has been born again.

I speak a blessing into your life and I pray that as you read this book, the Lord will speak to your heart, bless your soul, and reveal things to you that bring comfort and peace.

Your Sister in Christ Jesus,

    b

Dedication

This work is lovingly dedicated to my Lord and Saviour, Jesus Christ.

Without You, I am nothing. I praise and thank You, Lord for Your ever keeping power, for your unspeakable gift of forgiveness, for Your mercy, Your grace, Your kindness, and Your all encompassing agape love.

Thank You, Lord, for never giving up on me and for the many wonderful people You have placed across my path in this life, the many mentors, and the wonderful, anointed, Godly man you blessed me with in my husband, Randy.

You are everything to me, My Lord.

I love You,

b

Invitation

Precious Brother and Sister,

It is no accident that you are reading this book. The Lord has made a way for you to receive this urgent invitation.

Please look into your heart, right now, and make a decision to receive the Lord, Jesus , as your personal Lord, Messiah, and Saviour. Admit that you have sinned, as the Word of God tells us that we all have sinned and fallen short of the glory of God, Romans 3:23.

Repent of your sin against God, Acts 3:19, and confess with your mouth the Lord Jesus and believe in your heart that God raised Him from the dead , Romans 10:9.

If you have said this prayer and believed it with your heart, you are born again. May I be the first to welcome you to your new heavenly family. I urge you to attend the Christian church that the Lord Jesus guides you to.

You are about to embark on the greatest adventure of your life. Welcome home,

b

Contents

Day 1	2
Day 2	4
Day 3	6
Day 4	8
Day 5	10
Day 6	12
Day 7	14
Day 8	16
Day 9	18
Day 10	20
Day 11	22
Day 12	24
Day 13	26
Day 14	28
Day 15	30
Day 16	32
Day 17	34
Day 18	36
Day 19	38
Day 20	40
Day 21	42
Day 22	44
Day 23	46
Day 24	48
Day 25	50
Day 26	52
Day 27	54
Day 28	56
Day 29	58
Day 30	60

Day 1

Anger is always a no win situation. I know you go through aggravating situations, but anger can only lead to sin and sin leads to death.

Have you read in My word…be angry and sin not…take not your own revenge…bless those that curse you…pray for those that despitefully use you?

Anger also leads to sickness. Some of My own children are suffering sickness because of their anger. Agree with your enemy quickly, loose and release them to Me, overcome evil with good.

To walk in constant forgiveness is to walk in constant health. Righteous anger is meant to correct a wrong, (such as the money changers in the temple). When Jesus walked this earth, there were many that came against Him, He prayed and set a consistent quiet time with Me to loose and release His cares.

Truly, you **must** give your cares to Me. I will make right what your enemies do to you. I see all, I know all, and yes, I am merciful to your enemies…to a point. If they do not repent, they will reap the harvest born of hurting you…not only that, but they will see My unlimited favor upon you. The more they attack, the more favor I will release.

Forgiveness is the key to having your enemies walk in peace with you. The physical body is meant to only carry a healthy amount of stress…a level that motivates you to action….but not so much that it makes you sick physically.

My people are under great stress right now and I hear their groanings…just as when they were in Egypt…and now just as then I will bring them out.

Day 2

Child, there are many things I want you to know. First, that My love is perfect and everlasting..that My mercy and grace truly are new for you every morning… that you mean so much to Me.

I will take you in some unusual and strange paths. There are some places and some people that only you can reach. I always prepare you before I send you. When you begin your ministry you will be well equipped…you will be able to completely trust Me.

I will temper (prepare) you in fiery trials first. You will learn to deal with attitudes and situations, first. I will humble you before I elevate you. I will allow hurts and disappointments to get you ready to be in the habit of turning to Me first.

I will repeat and repeat painful experiences until you learn My way to deal with them. This is why some are stuck at different levels of their training (preparations) …they do not allow Me to do the work I need to in order to prepare them for the ministry I created them for.

Each one has a plan and a purpose. Every vessel has an anointing and a measure of faith. Faith grows through trials…humility through disappointments. I will never allow frustration to the point of breaking one's spirit, but I do allow tempering to reach the final goal.

Stubbornness and anger only put you back into training. Submission and repentance allow you to move onwards. Submit quickly…move up to the next level quickly.

Can anyone fight My will? My purpose? (like a fish struggling in a net) It is useless and will only exhaust you.

Trust and submission…this is pleasing to Me.

Day 3

Expect something wonderful…so many of Mine expect bad things to happen…they receive and believe bad reports from doctors…they don't expect promotion or provision or prosperity and all these things have already been promised and paid for.

Redemption not only bought back souls, but all things needed in this earthly realm. I know you have need of money, shelter, clothing, cars. I have provided for this. You have not because you receive not.

If you ask me…it's My pleasure to give… My great pleasure. But remember, it will be according to My perfect timing. I will not leave…I will not forsake…I will not withhold what is needful to My children. They are blessed in all the earth.

I am still protecting and providing as I did for the Israelites in the desert…a cloud by day and a pillar of fire by night. My children are impatient. They want to lead and direct me—NOT SO. Those who wait upon Me shall mount up as eagle's wings. Wait, I say, wait upon the Lord.

Blessings have been missed because My people won't wait…they settle for less than I intended for them. Have I not said…NEVER the less? My people should stand out…prosperous, healthy, wise…they are My representatives. But instead, they are poor, blind, and naked.

When will you learn… when will you listen…when will you wait upon Me ? I long to bless My children, but I will not throw pearls before swine. WAIT patiently and gain wisdom.

Day 4

It's true, these are the days I will pour out My Spirit upon all men…all who believe in Me and call out and follow Me. Gifts of Healing and Deliverance and Prophesy will flow as never before.

My people will be warned and corrected as never before. Things have been loosed in the earth---evil things---that the world has never seen…but My strength and My power has also been released as never before.

Those who have an ear to hear Me will make it through the coming disasters. Many will lose hope and give up. I am always near… as near as your next heartbeat, but some will miss Me and My warnings, My power anyway. You **must** spend time with Me in order to know My voice.

The enemy is subtle; he will mix scripture with truth. Have I not said that the end time is cut off early so the very elect will not fall? My sheep **must** know My voice for there are wolves in sheep's clothing just waiting to lead them astray.

Beware of "new" revelations of My Word that don't line up with it. My Word confirms itself. I have made your spirit man to receive a check when things do not agree with or line up with My Word.

You must draw nigh to Me as never before. Dangers and temptations abound. It's becoming worse than the days of Noah…one of the biggest deceptions is that you are safe because I delay My coming.

My true servants will be mocked and persecuted for their fervent pleas to repent and return to Me. Believe Me, the time is very short now and My Word **must** come to pass.

I will that none should perish…hell is real…but each one has free will to choose their eternal resting place.

Day 5

*J*oy and anger cannot abide in the same place at the same time. Anger is detrimental to your health…spirit, soul, and body. It leads to hatred which leads to sin (murder).

Joy can be had in spite of your circumstances…you can have peace in a storm (calm)…this is much different from happiness …which depends on what's going on.

I will that My people have joy that is full, complete. In the midst of trials I will send joy unspeakable to help you bear through it. Joy gives strength…it has healing properties…like a bubbling fountain on the inside that cannot be stopped.

Joy is a replenisher while anger saps all your energy. One heals…one destroys. I would that My people be full of joy at **all** times. They need only ask.

Joy is something desperately needed in theses times. Another replenisher is speaking in tongues…and it is a (spiritual) weapon… a way for our spirits to commune on a deeper level…a way to come into My presence. Tongues are for this time, when demonic attacks are great…there is a much greater need to be in My presence.

Darkness and light cannot occupy the same space and when you are in My presence…you are in the light. Darkness understands it not…confuse the enemy by coming into My presence in the midst of your trials. Anger will try to have you blame Me and be separated… but this is when you need Me the most.

Many turn away from Me in trials when this is the very thing intended to bring them closer to Me… to show others where strength can be found and renewed.

Day 6

To be sure, the devil is moving, but remember where sin and evil abounds, My grace abounds more. My grace is the strength you need to fight the enemy. My way **will** be done; there is no way to stop My plan.

Everything has been orchestrated. Even the evil that is now in the world…I have planned it. This is the time for the greatest outpouring of My Spirit on earth. Miracles that have not been seen since the time of the book of Acts will happen and are happening even now.

Yet in the midst of even these, the faith of some will wax cold. Many will give up on the miracles they've been praying and waiting for just as they are about to happen because of discouragement and impatience.

I will reign miracles on the just and the unjust to verify to all that I alone am the Lord and there is none like Me. Some will choose to not believe even when a miracle happens right in front of them.

They will reason and attribute it to luck, chance, etc. Even now, I am moving in the earth as never before. Many will come to know Me and be saved. Never doubt that hell is a real place…a place of pain and torment…a place of darkness devoid of My presence.

The angels that fell are full of hate and violence and take joy in their torture of lost souls. Truly, hell does enlarge herself by the day. The torments there are as indescribable as the joys of heaven.

I grieve for every soul that denies Me and chooses to go there. At the same time, there is great joy for each one that chooses to believe in Me.

Day 7

*D*ivine protection is given to those who will listen and wait. I will protect the impatient, but not to the same degree.

My Word says to be slow to speak...not to do. Blessings are for those who obey quickly. I know My requests may sometimes seem strange, but My ways are not your ways.

Jesus heard and obeyed and that's what I expect of My people. Remember that I am coming soon. I look upon men's hearts...I know their real motives and intentions. The Father has angels that record such things.

Many do the right things with hearts full of deceit... wanting man to see and glorify them, while others will silently endure hardship after hardship and only I know what they're going through....these will be blessed by Me.

Remember that human appreciation is very fickle... here today; gone tomorrow... that is why it is better to obey God than man. Even Jesus got cheers one day (riding in on a donkey) and jeers and insults the next (going to the cross..."crucify Him").

The crucifixion was the most cruel, painful, slowest way to die that man had. Jesus endured **every** type of abuse and shame, and yet obeyed. Some of Mine have learned to obey, but it is no good without the right motive.

Obedience must be quick and out of love and trust. I take no pleasure in obedience done out of habit. I don't want to be another thing you check off your list.

Come to Me with reverence, with humility, and with a right heart.

My throne room is always open and I never sleep.

Day 8

The end times are upon the earth even now. Pestilence, wars, famines, rumors of wars are here now. There is no way to tell the seasons by the weather. People are acting the same as in the days of Noah.

There is no fear of Me…no reverence. Warnings of the coming disasters are being ignored…but the wrath in the cups **will** be poured out…the horsemen will ride to the four corners of the earth.

I will come in the clouds and later I will stand on the Mount of Olives. This earth will pass away…a new earth will be born.

With all the knowledge accessible today…many will miss the very information they need to save their souls from hell. They will go to hell greatly educated in the things of this world thinking that their intellect is greater than their need for salvation. What does it profit man if he gains the world and loses his soul?

Eternity is a long, long time…bitterness, unforgiveness; (even of yourself) rejection of the blood sacrifice of Jesus…aught (grievance) against each other will keep you out of the heavenly home meant for you.

Now is the time to forgive, **now** is the time to love your enemies, **and now** is the time to receive salvation… **right now.**

I am loving and merciful, but I will not strive with man forever and My wrath is sure.

I would that none would perish…but I know that many will choose it. The lust of the eyes, the lust of the flesh, and the pride of life will keep many from choosing Me.

Day 9

Fresh water and old should not be coming from the same source. Just so, My people must choose whom they will serve. (Me on Sunday…the devil the rest of the week.) A good witness has one master.

The tongue is amazing in that it has not only the power of life and death, but also the power to heal and act right. Ah, but it is **very** hard to tame.

My followers have yet to tame it. It is full of wickedness and deceit. My people need to learn how important it is to speak forth the right thing with the right attitude.

I ask more of you as you are going through (trials) so you can see where you're **really** at, spiritually. Many thought they were holy until tested in the trials of adversity…then they are able to see their real selves. Your real self is revealed by what you do and say while under pressure.

My people will do My will for time is short and I will soon come back to claim My own. Those found without spot or blemish will go home with Me. Those who are not yet ready will cry out for mercy and receive it.

Some will **never** believe or receive. These are destined to hell. They will teach their wicked precepts from hell. They will cry out for mercy and it will be too late.

I will have you to warn some, to get their attention. The light will shine before them, but it's up to them to follow the light.

Those who choose to follow, choose life everlasting. Those who choose not to follow, choose eternity in hell.

I will tug at the hearts of men, but I will not choose for them.

Day 10

Complacency among My people is making them lazy. As long as things go well in their lives...as long as nothing is happening to them or their family...they are content to sit and wait for eternity in heaven.

But the church is meant to care for its members... meant to hurt with those who are hurting, meant to be moved to the point of prayer, fasting, travail, for those who have needs.

Saved to serve and **not to sit.**

When Jesus walked the earth, He knew He would be going back to heaven. He could have easily sat back and waited, but He, as the church today, recognized the urgency of helping those in need...physically, spiritually, emotionally...even financially (coin in fish's mouth).

You have power from on high to demonstrate the awesome work of Almighty God right now, right here. This is not so people can look at other people and lift them up...but so the God of all creation can be recognized and glorified.

He is worthy of **ALL** praise at **ALL** times.

The angels are perplexed at times at the way God is treated so lightly….how He is taken for granted. He does not even owe us our next breath and no one is guaranteed tomorrow.

Saints are going home early because had they stayed, they would have strayed away…that is mercy. Did I not say that I would that you be either cold or hot, but if you are luke warm; I will spit you from My mouth?

Love Me as I love you, with a passionate love, a love that grows ever stronger, a love that does not wax and wane.

Day 11

My power will be manifested in the earth in these end times as never before. It will be seen in the weather (tornados, earthquakes, hurricanes) and in healings as never before (limbs and organs will be restored, blind eyes will open, the deaf will hear, cancers will disappear).

This is the time of "greater works" (spoken of in the book of John). Many will come to know Me and receive Me…a great revival. There will also be great prejudice and harassment for My own.

This is the beginning of persecutions for Christians, and it will only get worse. My people will have to walk very closely to Me; they will have to know My Word for themselves…for they will be challenged every day. They must walk blameless and they must walk in love.

The enemy will attack on every side…at the same time I will give new (spiritual) weapons…love and humility, an attitude of serving…a soft word breaketh the bone and turns away wrath.

The enemy will say, " Look what is going on…how can your God allow this…does He even care…where is He now ?"

Yet, I will be as close to My own as their next breath…they will be protected and provided for…they will not be harmed by the calamities that surround them…as in Goshen when the Israelites and their families were spared in the midst of all the things (plagues) rained down on the Egyptians.

Persecution for My sake will be everywhere and is here, even now. This is a prelude to My return…a time of great sorrow and a time of great expectation. I will give My own joy in spite of their circumstances.

Day 12

I will speak again of things to come. There is a revival of the church coming that the world has never seen before. Many, many will be saved, healed and delivered. At the same time many will have their faith wax cold.

Counterfeit miracles will abound…that is why you **must** study My Word…to know the real true miracles from the counterfeit ones…especially the healings that will occur…Mine will be healed completely and permanently…the counterfeit will heal and the sickness will recur.

People of high intelligence (MDs, etc.) will attribute some of My healings to luck, circumstance, happenstance, spontaneous remission of disease…or to something man has done (medical treatment). Woe unto him who takes My glory…they will experience the same disease they have claimed to heal.

A one world global community is being formed even now… one world government, one world economy, one world religion. Woe unto them that accept this. My Word warns of these things. Even now, there are ID chips being developed for insertion in a person's hand that will contain general, medical, and financial information.

But I will always make a way for My remnant to have what they need without succumbing to the plan of the evil one. No matter what it looks like…I **AM** in control…I know My own and their protection and provision is sure.

My own will not lack…and if they can receive it… they will be prosperous. Piety does not go hand in hand with lack.

My holy ones will walk in the abundance meant for them.

Day 13

Let us speak of hope...hope gives strength to the weary...strength to carry on in diverse trials. A person without hope is like a dry and brittle bone...easily broken and completely depleted.

The enemy will try desperately to take away hope. Faith and hope work hand in hand...faith believes the unseen...hope gives strength to stand until faith is made visible. The world sorely needs hope right now.

If there is no hope, there is no reason to reconcile and work together. A people without hope will surely die...they will give up...dry up...waste away. It is better to be angry than to lose hope...there is passion and life in anger. Faith in Jesus Christ and hope in life eternal is strength for living.

Joy also works with hope...even if there is only a little hope...joy can be found. Joy goes beyond strength... it's a bubbling force that renews the spirit. Joy to the spirit is like food to the body.

Hope , joy, and faith will bring many through the trying times yet to come. They give supernatural strength and restoration to the spirit. The spirit man must be healthy for the physical body to be healthy.

Many of My own though affected by physical ailments are yet kept because of their spirit which is healthy.

All that you require is found in My presence. The cares of this world fade when you're in My presence. Those who make a habit of spending time with Me will walk in health and strength and My power will be manifested in their lives.

Day 14

Peace soothes the spirit and mind and allows the physical body to relax enough to receive healing. Whenever you pray for a physical healing for someone, pray also for peace of mind.

Peace is a rare and precious commodity now. If you do not have peace…you will not have physical rest (trouble sleeping) and your body will become weak and susceptible to all kinds of sickness and disease. But I will keep in perfect peace whose mind is stayed on Me.

Fear works to take peace away…worry and doubt work to take peace away. If you give in to these because of what you see, what you hear, what you feel… your body is in jeopardy of becoming sick…are not the hospitals full of people whose disease started in the mind (worry, doubt, fear) and became physical manifestations…gastric problems, heart problems, cancer. Yes, cancer can start from fear…fear of lack of finances, fear of what will happen on the job or to your children.

Fear, worry and doubt trigger stress…this depletes the natural mechanism placed in your body to heal and repair itself, the immune system. Your body is meant to self repair, not receive drug after drug which in itself creates other/new problems.

Have I not said, "Cast your cares upon Me?" Have I not told you how to keep your mind free from fear, worry, and doubt …take every thought captive…keep your mind stayed on Me…guard your mind…think on things that are lovely, noble, good (Phil 4).

Your mind is very powerful and has the creative power to heal or allow disease…choose life…choose Me.

I would that you prosper **AND BE IN HEALTH** even as your soul prospers.

Day 15

Contentment with godliness is great gain. To be content in whatever your circumstances are is to have peace of mind. You cannot have lack when you are content, because whether you have a little or a lot, it **is** enough…therefore there is no lack.

To covet is the opposite of being content with who you are and what you have. This comes from comparing yourself to someone else. I have made you…each of you…unique and special…you all have anointings and ministries…yet you reject that which you have and covet that which you have not. What a waste of time!

To covet is to be ungrateful with what you have been given. To covet what someone else has will only bring anxiety, frustration, and jealousy. Each one's gifts are meant to work together…to be given to each other to build the Kingdom of God.

How can you be a Preacher when you have a Prophet's anointing? How can you be a Psalmist with a Teacher's anointing? Let each one go forth in their **own** gifts. Seek to please **ME**. Too many want the praise of men…NOT SO.

Even if no one understands your ministry, go forth in it because it pleases **ME**. It is better to obey God than man. Remember that man's favor is fickle…you will gain it one day and lose it the next.

Please **ME**…I do not change. Jealousy is a divider among men and I want My own to be united. Jealousy leads to anger which leads to rage which leads to murder.

Be content where you are, who you are, with your anointing. To be ungrateful is to be out of My will.

Every ministry is important in My eyes. Trust Me in My choice for you.

Day 16

Strength is found as you speak forth My Word. It has power to change things. When the Word is spoken, things begin to happen in the spiritual realm. Soon after, things change in the physical realm.

Prayer can be likened to a seed…this seed is watered (fed) by faith. Once it starts to grow results will be seen in the physical. Prayer touches My very heart. Prayer takes humility…the act of admitting that only I can change things.

There are many powerful life changing prayers in My Word. Make no mistake…they are NOT a magic formula to produce a desired effect…but words with power that are intended to be spoken with reverence and humility.

Faith takes submission…the act of waiting on Me for whatever you need for whatever length of time it takes to manifest in the physical. I look on your heart… your attitude MUST be right when speaking to Me.

A humble and submitted heart moves Me. The effectual fervent prayer of the righteous man truly does avail much…miracles have happened because of faith and submission.

Anger and an attitude of entitlement will create a distance between us. You know not the plans set forth for you…the road you will travel on this earth is not guaranteed to be trouble free. To the contrary, adversity must come to shape you into the one that I intended you to be before you were even born.

Be assured that each one's life is carefully planned before their first breath is drawn. Stubbornness and rebellion will halt My plan for you…but repentance will bring you back to right standing.

Day 17

Let us speak of prayer and fasting. Fasting is the way to bring the physical body under subjection…to purify the thoughts…to become humble. Those who make a regular habit of fasting will hear Me clearly.

There are times when I will call a fast for a specific reason in a church…this unites the church and makes way for My presence and My power to manifest in a supernatural way.

Fasting, when done in obedience to Me, will break the yokes and bring deliverance to those who fast for the right reason and with the right attitude. Just as with giving…with praise…with obedience…fasting must be done the way I intended…with the right attitude of the heart.

Fasting and prayer are powerful together…this is the way to break down strongholds to bring deliverance from demonic attacks. Fasting will bring you into My presence and where **I am**…demons must flee.

Darkness and light cannot occupy the same space. Fasting is a purifier…for the spirit…for the body…for the mind. Fasting is not something done only by the early church, but is meant for My people right now.

Things will be activated in the spirit realm as the flesh submits and stands humbly before Me. Jesus fasted often and I sustained Him with "food" for His spirit man that His Apostles knew not.

Fasting during trials strengthens the spirit man (Jesus in the desert). The body is meant to be purified during seasons of fasting. Fasting as a church is a unifying force and when My people stand united according to My Word, I will withhold no good thing from them, but move quickly on their behalf.

Day 18

Complaining, grumbling, and murmuring will all take you away from your blessings and delay your blessings…they are the opposite of trust and faith. Without faith…apart from believing what I say is true…you **cannot** please Me.

I only ask that when you pray…when you are given a prophetic word…believe it and receive it right away. My timing is not your timing and you may have to wait for a while…even years…for it to manifest in the physical…but My Word is sure.

I cannot lie…My Word will not come back void, but will accomplish that which I sent it to do. No matter what things look like My Word is sure.

Imagine what the Israelites thought as the Egyptians pursued them into the Red Sea…but they saw victory over their enemies that day and were never again pursued or persecuted by that enemy.

Instead of complaining, which delays your blessing, thank Me and confess and agree with My Word that your blessing will happen. When you and I are in agreement…the blessings will flow…this is when I open up the windows of heaven and pour out.

Thank me in all things at all times… this is My will for you. Did I not say rejoice always? Your attitude must be one of joyful expectation (like a child opening a gift).

My Word is sure…My will is to bless and prosper you…but you must have the right attitude in your heart.

You must remember, hold on to, and confess the prophesies said over you… they will and must come to pass.

My plans for you are good and not evil, but many times you will need to wait upon them. Believe Me, things are being arranged and orchestrated in ways you cannot see from the moment My promise is given.

Day 19

Blessings are about to flow in the earth as never before. There will be miracles and healings that the world has not seen. Yes…there will be terrible things…wars, famines, pestilence, cruelty…but there will also be supernatural moves and provisions and interventions.

My people will be delivered from the attacks of their enemies. The more they attack…the more I will bless My people…My faithful ones. Faith in times of trial (the sacrifice of faith) deeply moves Me, and will not go unrewarded.

You will be rewarded in this time, in this earth. Many of My own do not think that blessings and rewards are for their time on earth…of course they are!

When you delight yourself in Me I **will** give you the desires of your heart. When you put Me first, blessings will flow. When you desire Me…love Me…obey Me first, I will pour out blessings.

I am full, so when you minister to Me, I automatically overflow…blessings will follow each one that delights themselves in Me.

Every good and great gift is from above…they were created to bless My people during their time on earth. The earth was originally created to be a place of great beauty, great peace…a place that reflected My glory and inspired My praise.

Even today I paint the skies and blow gentle winds…did you see or stop to appreciate what I painted for you today?

I whisper words of beauty and kindness and love…did you hear them today?

Ministering angels walk the earth to serve Me…to protect My own…were you blessed by one of them today?

Like the wind…even though you cannot see Me…I constantly surround you and the evidence of My presence is ever with you.

Day 20

The devil and his fallen angels roam the world seeking whom they may deceive and devour. They entice, they tempt, they lie, they cheat, they steal…they have a murderous spirit.

Know this…they **cannot** do anything without permission. Why do you think they pose as angels of light and wolves in sheep's clothing? They are masters at deception.

They mix outright lies with the truth in My Word. Again I say…they can do nothing without permission… they must gain access to a willing individual and consent is assumed when a person partakes of their offerings….occult practices and games , tarot and card readings, palm and tea readings, horoscope readings… willing worship to any other god but Me…revenge, gossiping, backbiting, coveting, jealousy, anger, rage.

When you partake, you open the door to; oppression, depression, possession, sickness, bondage, and all evil things.

Learn to stay in My presence and to declare My Word to the hurting souls (deliverance). Keep your thoughts and your words pure…walk in forgiveness…repent quickly…walk in love.

Your spirit man wants to follow Me, but the flesh is truly weak. Strengthen your physical body through prayer and fasting…partake (regularly) of the Lord's Supper. My body was given to bring you health, salvation and deliverance.

Know ye not that ye are the temple of the Holy Spirit purchased at a great price?

Temples should be clean…holy…pure…a place prepared and kept for the Holy Spirit to dwell in.

Don't grieve Me by taking the blood sacrifice of the spotless lamb, Jesus Christ, lightly.

Day 21

*C*hild, let your tears flow…don't ever be ashamed to cry out to Me. I am as close as your next breath, your next heartbeat, and I want you to cast all your cares upon Me.

No matter how it feels, I am working this out for your good and no, I will not give you more than you can bear.

Remember the goldsmith how, when he is refining the gold to remove impurities he cannot…even for a second…take his eyes off the gold…to stop too soon is to leave impurities and to stop too late is to let the gold break down. The timing must be perfect …must be done by a master goldsmith.

I will not let you go through to the point of breaking your spirit…neither will I let up until the refining removes that which is impure. Trials show you weak spots…things that need to be changed and let go of in your life.

Do not despise the refining for this is how you are molded into the one that I intend you to be. And yes, during the trying times of refining, I will require you to minister to others, to show My love in the midst of your own hard times. This is the breaking…where you are decreased and I am increased…some give up too soon and have to go through the refining process over and over.

Cry out to Me, trust Me, pray to Me, but do not give up when in the refining fire for pure gold is about to manifest …strength and joy and blessings are waiting to overtake you.

I am with you, I am for you, I will not leave you for you are My very own purchased with a precious price.

Salvation is free, but to walk in your anointing and appointed ministry many trials will be endured for refining and purifying must be done.

Day 22

Trusting Me is something you must learn…this is done through trials. When I deliver you from your afflictions, you learn to trust Me. The problem is that after the deliverance, My people soon forget what I have done for them.

To develop humility, trials will happen over and over. Humility…understanding that you can do nothing apart from Me…this is pleasing to Me. I hate a haughty spirit and an attitude of (self) pride.

Humility leads to trust which leads to faith. Faith… waiting and believing (on Me)…pleases Me. Pride comes before the fall and humility before honor. This is why some of My people have not yet been elevated… their spirits have not developed humility.

To elevate someone with a haughty spirit is to set them up for a fall. You cannot go forth in your anointing or your ministry in the way I intended without humility.

Jesus was a humble and meek servant. Remember that meekness does not in any way mean weakness. For meekness is strength under control…the ability to keep silent when being attacked by the enemy…the ability to forgive, loose and release in the midst of fiery trials.

In order to go to the next (higher) level you must learn obedience by staying humble through adversity. It's tempting to give in to anger and self pity, but these will only allow you to repeat the same lessons over and over.

I see every tear, I hear every thought, I see the attitude of men's hearts behind the false humility that they display. Anger and rage are not only damaging to the spirit and soul, but to the physical body.

You cannot be My ambassadors and display godly attitudes while harboring anger. Loose and release your frustrations to Me quickly and I will give you peace.

Day 23

Contentment with godliness is great gain...do you know why? Contentment is a choice you make to accept who you are, what you have and whatever circumstances you find yourself in...to choose to be satisfied.

How many times have I told you not to compare yourself with others? Each is given their own path... their own trials...their own blessings. Your life was planned out just for you. To not be content with what I have given you is to be ungrateful.

To envy or covet what someone else has can only lead to frustration, anxiety, anger and jealousy. Lack of self control has many of My own in financial debt and overweight physically. They are tired and worn out chasing things that I would gladly give them if they only waited on Me to do so.

I see the desires of your heart...and I will gladly give it to you **IF** you delight in Me...if you put Me first... if you desire Me more than the things of this earth... don't you realize that they are only temporary?

The most beautiful objects on this earth will eventually rot away. The yearning and emptiness you try to fill was meant for a Holy treasure…a relationship with Me. That will fulfill and satisfy and complete you. The void you feel cannot be satisfied with food, sex, clothes, cars or any temporary thing on this earth.

Delight yourself in Me. Don't you know that I long to have an intimate relationship with all My children? My love is not comparable to the love between a man and a woman or the love of brothers and sisters…My love is deep…My love is wide…My love sent Jesus to the cross.

Put Me first and you will be well satisfied and I will give you the desires of your heart.

Day 24

My daughter, like Martha, you are troubled by many things. First, know this, that I am for you and if I am for you…**who** can be against you? I hold the hearts of men in My hands and I turn them whither so ever way I will. Nothing shall by any means hurt you and yes, this battle belongs to Me.

Leave room for the wrath of God…vengeance is Mine…I will repay. I require that you confess your sin, that you bless those that curse you, and pray for those that despitefully use you.

Loose and release your troubles to Me for I am well able to fix what is wrong. Do not worry, do not fret, be anxious for nothing for I am with you always…you are My very own…I will not leave or forsake you.

Praise Me now because there is a wonderful blessing waiting for all who put their trust in Me. This too shall pass…have I not said it? Trust Me, dear one, I hold you in the palm of My hand.

Times of trials and tribulations must come, but they will not last. This is the time to submit and surrender… your enemies cannot do anything unless I allow it. Lift up your countenance for My joy is your strength.

To see you acting victorious, to hear you praise Me, to know your faith is in Me, this gives Me joy which in turn, gives you strength.

The enemy is busy and more cruel and devious than ever. At the same time, My power in the earth is greater than ever.

Do not ever doubt that I am in control…that the earth and the fullness thereof belong to Me. I am for you, trust Me.

This too shall pass.

Day 25

*D*id I not tell you that the best is yet to come? When you release your faith...I release My blessings. Blessings and miracles are yet to come. Trust Me always.

If you will only stop and listen, I will speak to you...doesn't My Word say, "to those who have a (spiritual) ear, let them hear." I have made My Word simple enough for a child to understand...don't make it complicated...I want you to read and understand.

My yoke is easy and My burden is light. I am here to fight your battles...when you cry, I'm there. When you praise, when you become still and listen for My voice, when you decide to step out in faith and trust Me...I'm there.

I will not leave my own even as a shepherd will not leave his sheep. I will correct you and direct you and I will chasten those whom I love...but I will not leave you. Only come to me with a willing and clean attitude of the heart. I cannot resist a humble and reverent heart.

No good thing will I withhold from those who truly love Me. Miracles and supernatural blessings are being poured out even now. All will know that I alone am God…there is none like unto Me.

I rule the waters, I blow the winds, I give and I take away. All souls will bow down before Me and receive their due recompense and reward.

Only mercy keeps the judgment until its due time. I would that each one receive Me but I know that some will not.

I have wept for those who have chosen hell over Me. Yet, free will allows each one to choose their place in eternity.

Day 26

*B*e still and know that I am God…I alone…there is none like unto Me. I am not some uncaring and distant ruler that is uninterested in My people. I cry when you cry, I laugh when you laugh, I hurt when you hurt.

I walked the earth in a flesh body…I was tempted in all the ways that you are. I have compassion and great love for each one I have created. You are made in My image…I have created each one to reflect My attributes.

Each one has been given distinct gifts and skills. Each one has a specific ministry. I was not always understood or welcomed when I walked the earth… neither will you be. Purpose in your heart to please Me and I will make a way for you with man.

Do what I ask regardless of how man may react… please Me and I will give you favor. Even your enemies will bless you and walk in peace with you…they won't understand why they're doing it…but they will do it none the less.

I want to fellowship, I want to revelate the deep things if only you will spend time with Me and listen.

This is a time of great knowledge…much information…the things that are most needful can be understood as you spend quiet time with Me.

Yes, I want to hear your prayers, but are you willing to wait long enough to hear My answers to them? I know what you will ask for before you say it…I asked you to let your requests be made known so we can fellowship…so there is communication not just from you to Me, but from Me to you.

Day 27

Let us speak of health and peace. I will keep in perfect peace whose mind is stayed on Me. There are so many pressures in the world today…so much stress. It creates an atmosphere of great mental turmoil.

People cannot sleep because their minds are racing…there is great unrest. If you cannot have peaceful rest, your physical body will suffer. You are meant and designed to heal and restore energy with physical rest.

I would that you seek Me when you cannot sleep…put away the pills; the alcohol…let Me give you true rest. There are always counterfeit ways to receive what you need, but My ways are better.

I will give My beloved sweet sleep. I will bless in great ways and add no sorrow to it. All that you need…I have it…just ask. You have not because you ask not. I want you to come to Me with all requests…I want you to come to Me with all decisions.

You can rest in Me. You can trust Me…even if I say No…it is to bring about good in your life. I see from beginning to end…I know the perfect timing to allow things to happen in your life.

You can go against My will, but your ways are not My ways and you will soon be praying to be delivered from what you have brought upon yourself.

Trust Me when I say that I love you, that I know the plans I have for you. Turn to Me often during the day…pray without ceasing.

Every day is planned, every day is filled with blessings…it's up to you to receive them or go your own way and miss them. I would that you follow My plan and be blessed.

Day 28

The devil and his angels want to constantly remind you of past sins and mistakes. Believe me when I tell you…if you repent from your heart and ask for forgiveness…**it's done.**

It's removed from you as far as the east is from the west. Forgiven sins are thrown into the sea of forgetfulness. When your mind is attacked…speak forth My Word. Use the sword of the Spirit to fight back…the devil himself cannot refute My Word and My word will **not** come back void…every time it is spoken things are set in motion in the spirit realm… battles are fought…strongholds are broken.

The enemy wants to shut your mouth…wants you to feel as though you are not worthy to speak My Word… you don't have to be worthy, you just have to be under the blood (of Jesus).

Use the shield of faith to protect your mind…faith believes Me only and not the lies and attacks from the enemy. When you speak forth the Word you increase your faith. Faith comes by hearing and hearing by the Word of God.

Want more faith? **Speak more of My Word.**

You will fall sometimes, make mistakes, miss the mark (sin)...that is why there was a perfect blood sacrifice...that is why you have an advocate (mediator)...that is why you have repentance...to get back into right standing with Me.

I know the flesh is weak, but let the weak say they are strong...I am your strength.

You have a high priest who prays for you at all times. Do not believe the enemy...take his power away by believing Me.

Day 29

Demonic attacks will not stop or prevent the miracles and blessings that are for this time...they will only bring My own closer to Me. They will serve to push My people closer than ever before. They will seek refuge in Me and I will deliver them from all evil.

Evil times are upon the earth. Things that would not have been tolerated even ten years ago are now common place. Anti-Christian attacks are common place. Israel is more of a target than ever before as are the countries that help her.

My beloved Israel will always have a remnant...will always have Divine protection and provision. As it goes in the Middle East...so goes the world.

Now is the time to focus on salvation...the things of this world will pass away...much quicker than you can imagine. People need salvation right now...pray for it...proclaim the Good News.

Be about the business of building the Kingdom... all such things that you need will be provided. I weep for each soul that does not receive salvation. Each one **MUST** hear so they can make a choice.

My people need to move now… the purpose of the church is to reach the lost. Many lives hang in the balance…many are in the valley of decision…the Gospel **MUST** reach all four corners of the world.

I have sent My own even to the remotest parts of the earth. All will know that I alone am God…that eternity is real…that hell is real…that each one **MUST** make a choice to receive or discard the blood sacrifice of the Spotless Lamb.

His sacrifice was beyond price and each one must know it.

Day 30

The day is coming soon when I will again set foot on this earth (for the last time). For this earth will pass away and there will be a new one and a New Jerusalem…that will be a time of great joy.

Even now the earth groans as the time of its passing draws near. The last days are a time of great tribulation…unprecedented changes in climate … great and terrible forces of nature…storms, winds, hurricanes, earthquakes, floods, famines, pestilence (diseases).

Yet, did I not say on the cross, "It Is Finished."? The future has been written in My Word. The steps have been orchestrated and circumstances have been set in motion.

Truly, time is short…the most urgent need is for salvation.

The Gospel is already on its journey around the world…oh, that the world would listen. The things of the devil…these people believe…there is fear of evil.

What you should fear is the One who can destroy your body and soul!

Where is the reverent fear of God? I will not strive with man forever. The time has been set and salvation is offered as a gift right now. To every thing is appointed a time and a season and the time for salvation is **now.**

Put away pride, put away anger, put away prejudice… speak My Word. Let people know that I'm alive and well and tell them the Good News of the Gospel.

I need living Epistles. How can one choose if they have not been given the choices?

Speak My Word.

Notes:_____

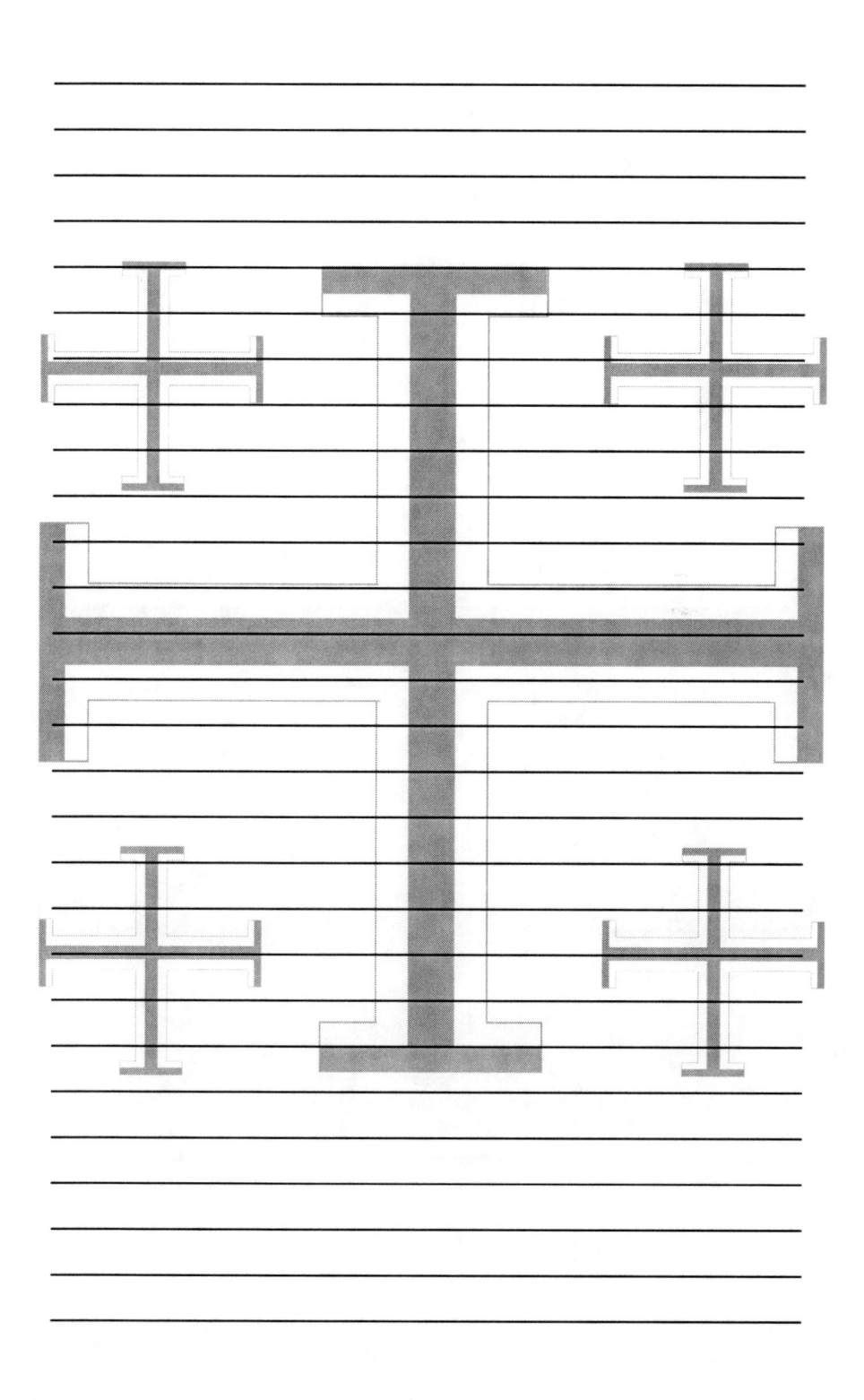

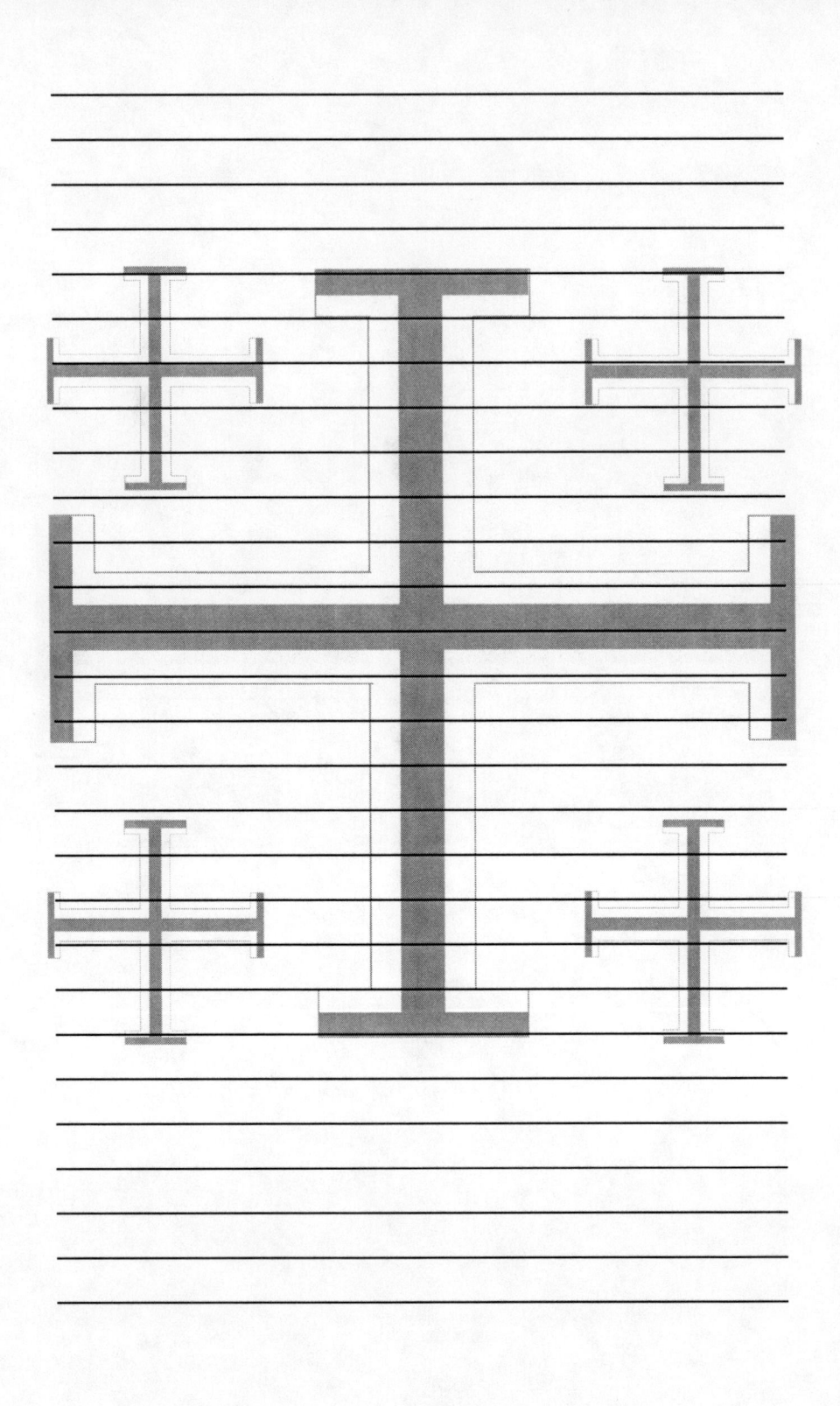

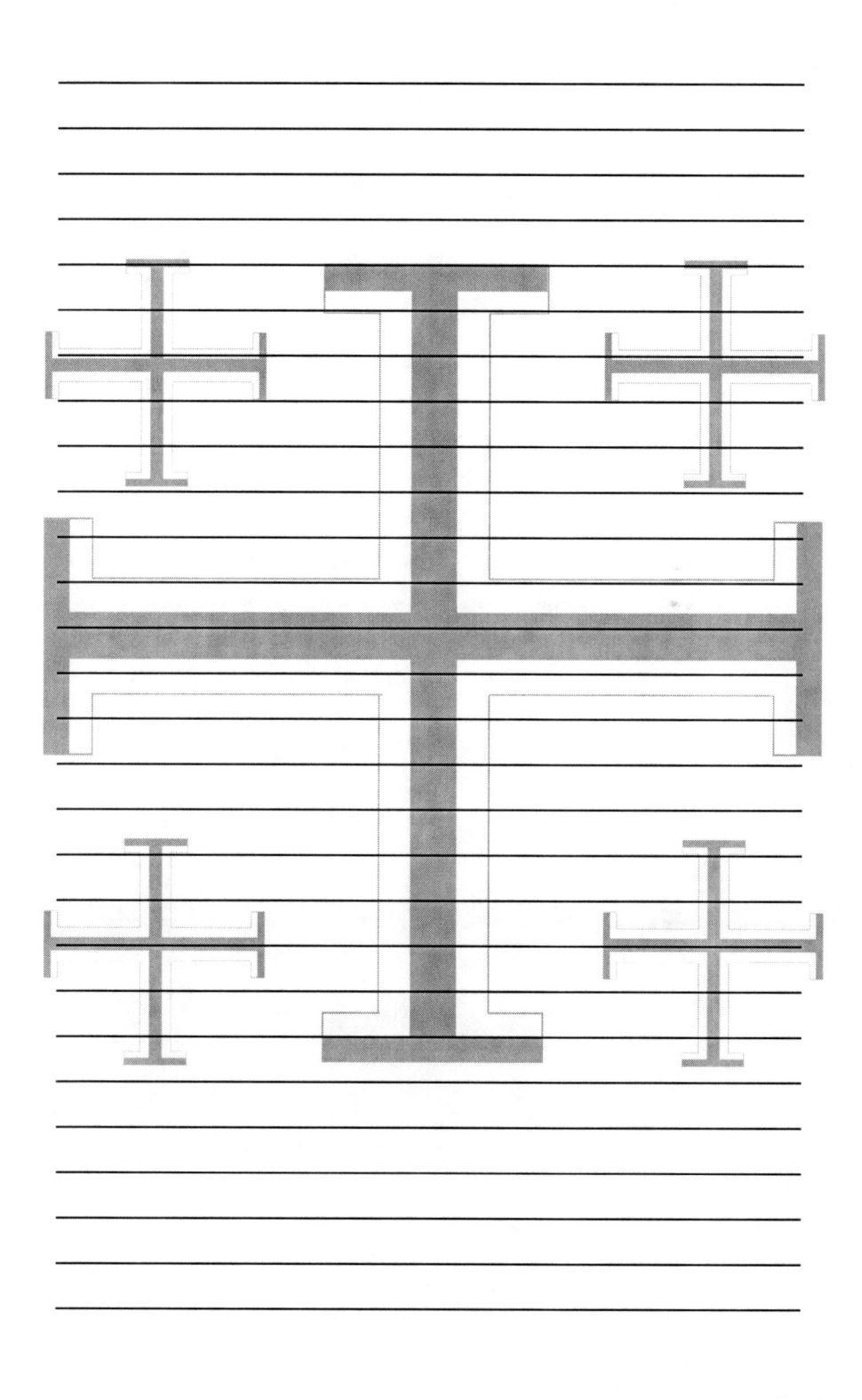

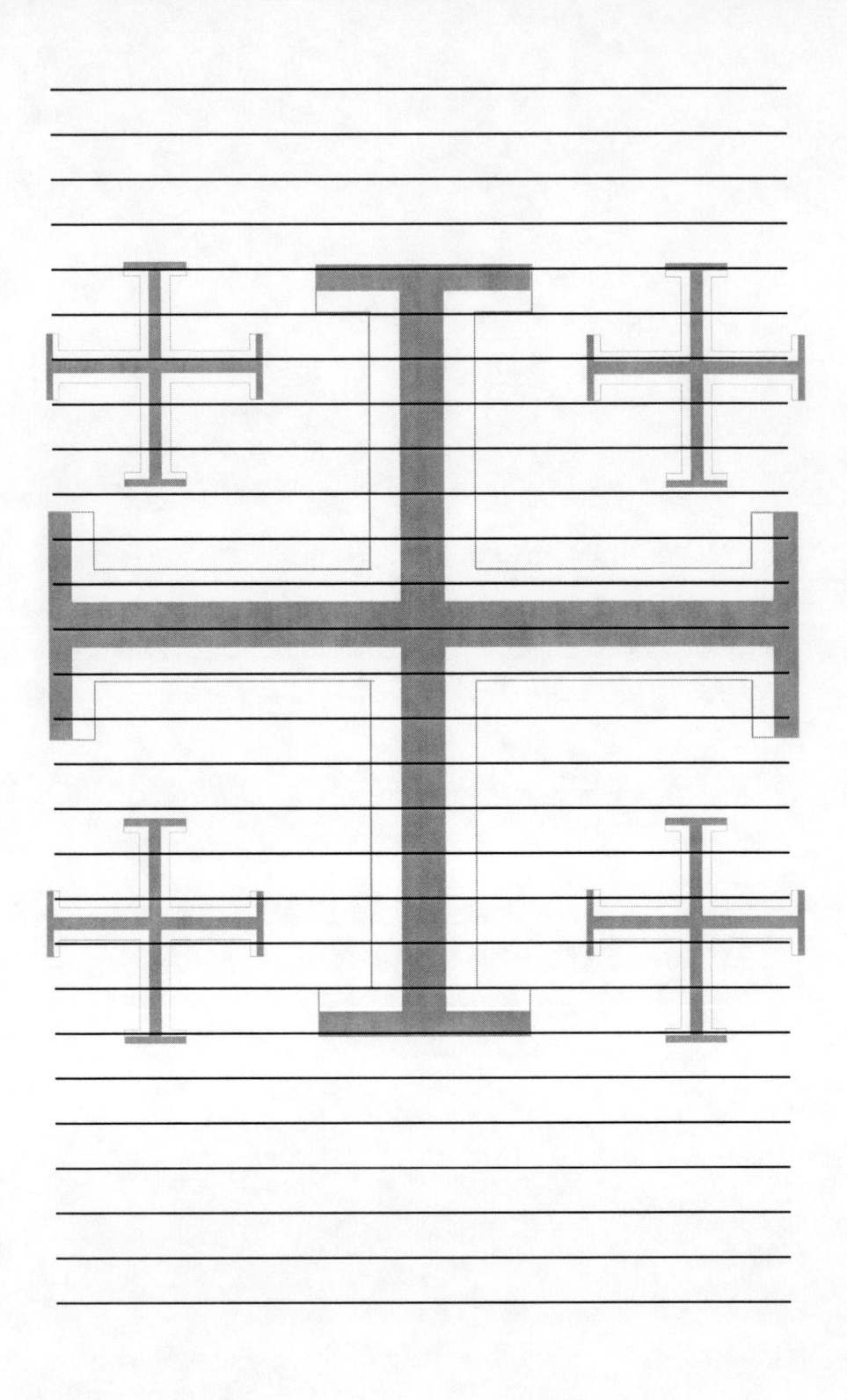

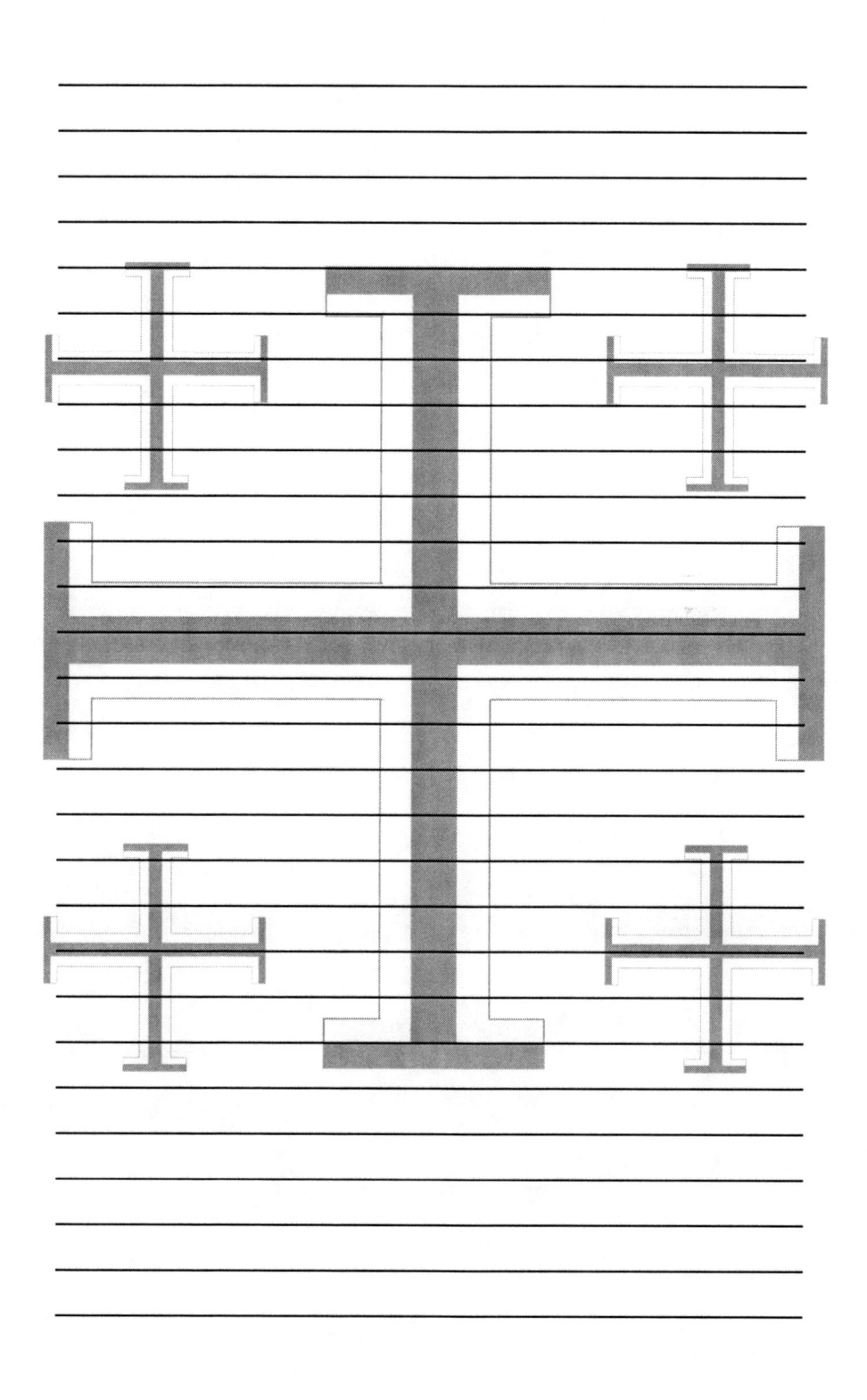

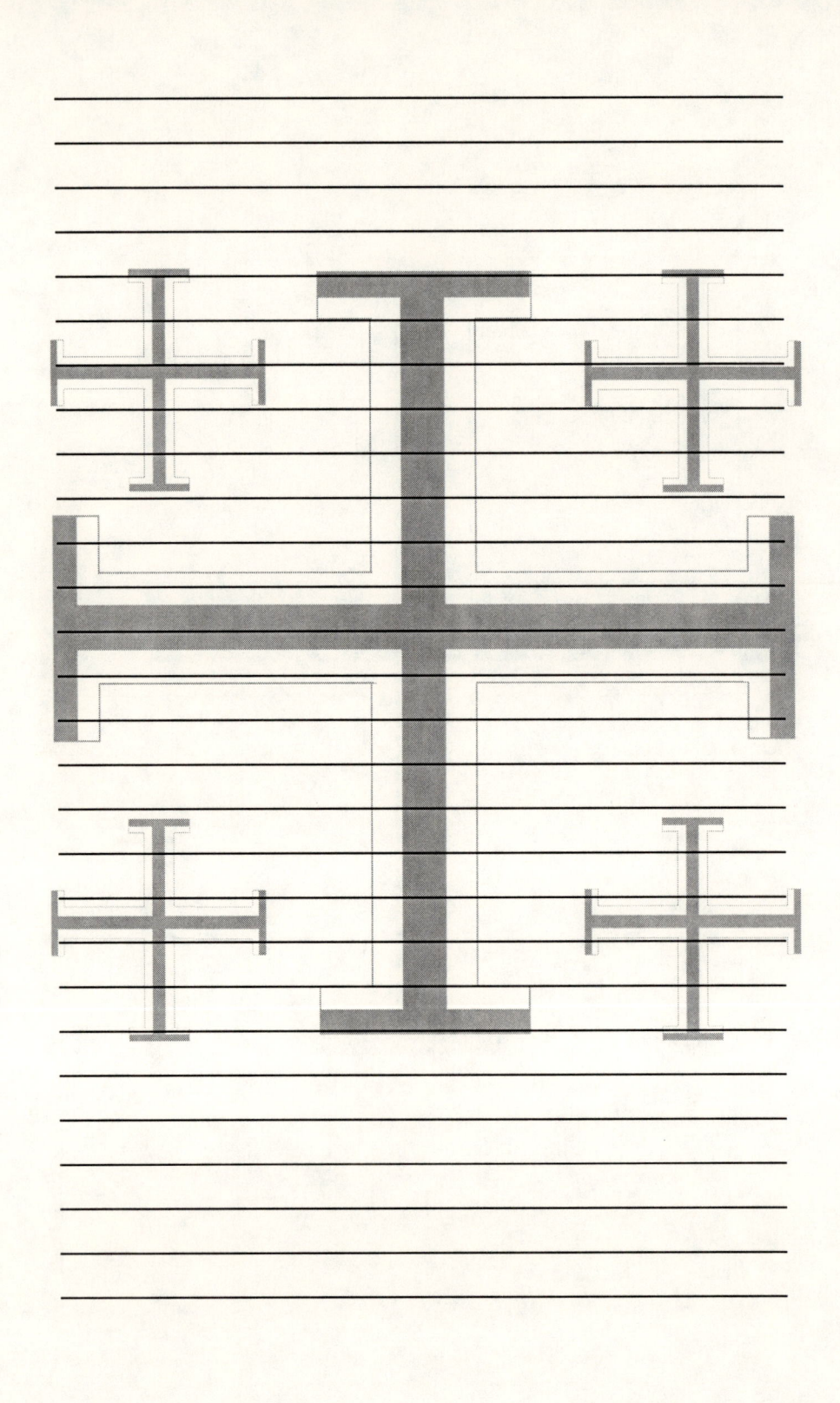

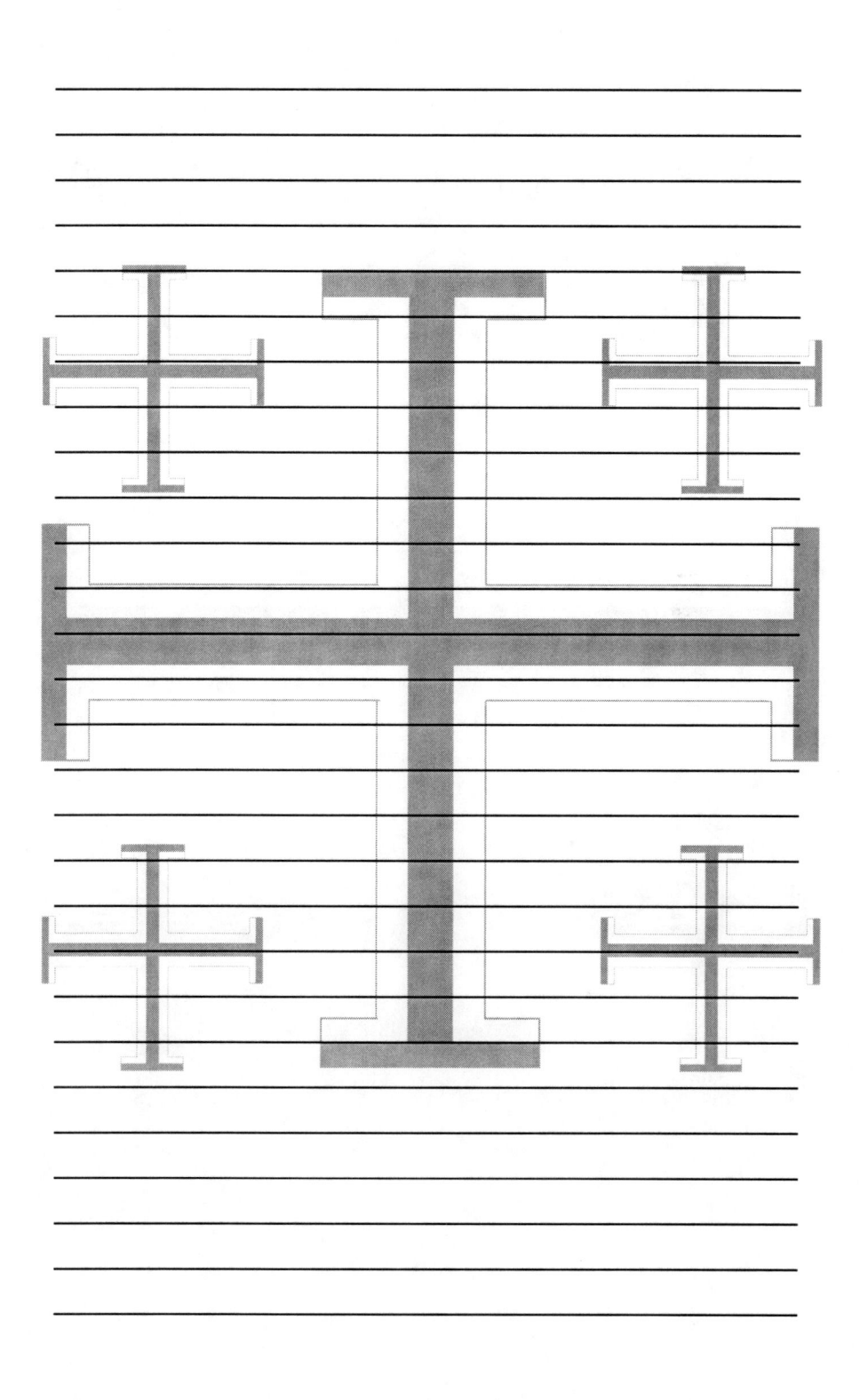

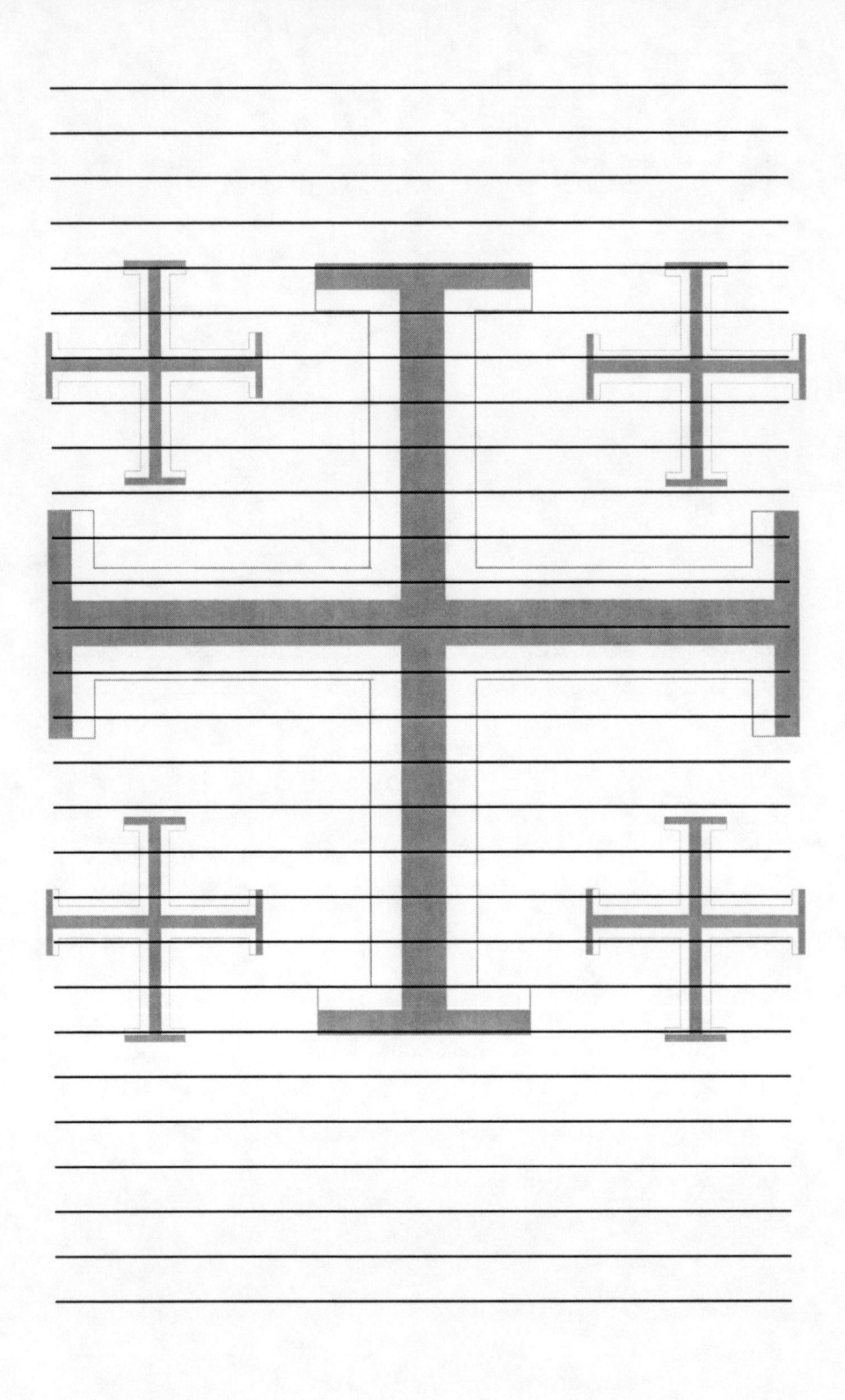

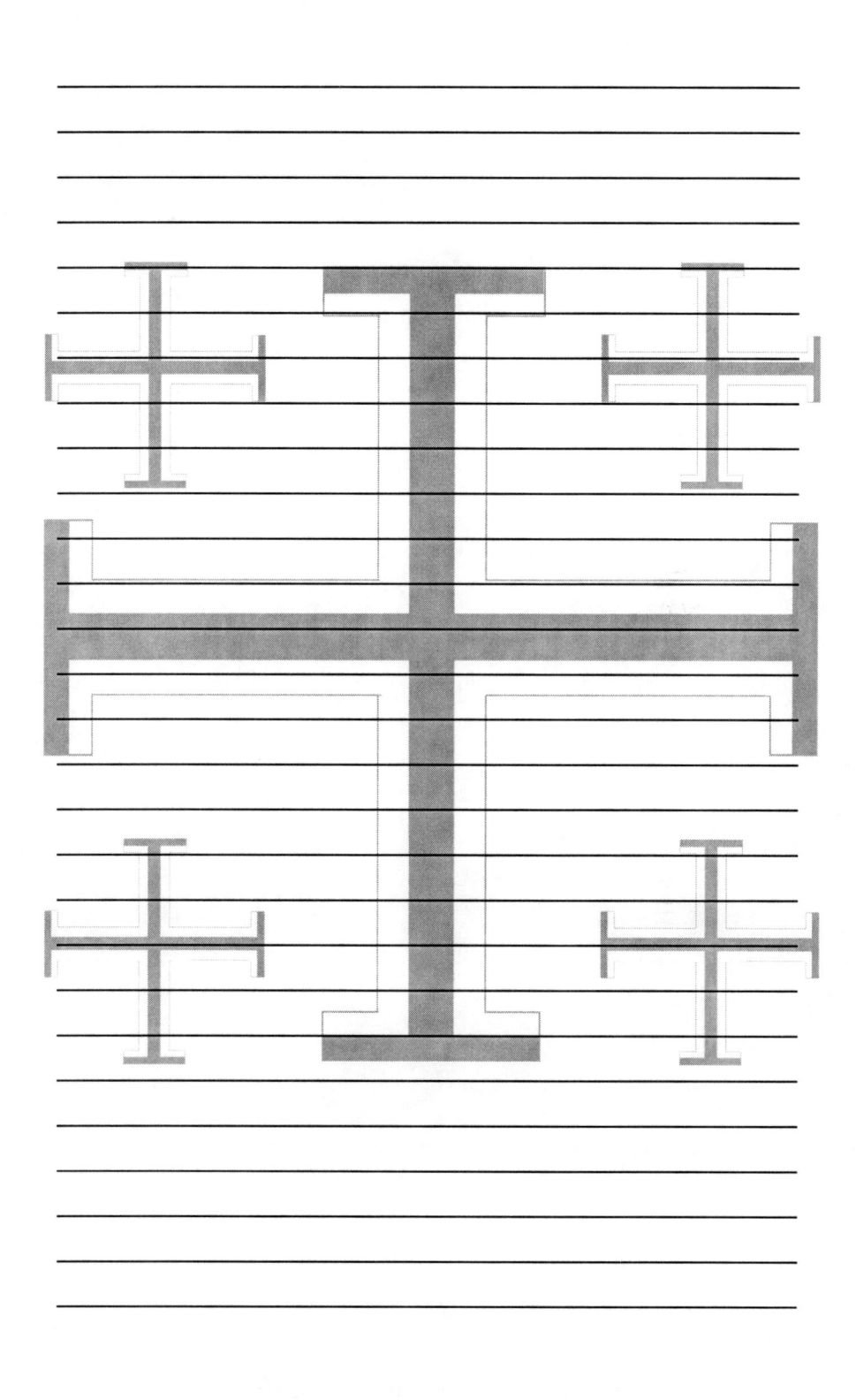

Printed in the United States
143724LV00004B/5/P